DISCARDED

Newsmakers™

Mahmoud Ahmadinejad

President of Iran

Matthew Broyles

ROSEN PUBLISHING®

New York

Dedicated to Nathan Broyles, with hope
for a bright world in which to grow

Published in 2008 by The Rosen Publishing Group, Inc.
29 East 21st Street, New York, NY 10010

First Edition

Library of Congress Cataloging-in-Publication Data

Broyles, Matthew.
Mahmoud Ahmadinejad: president of Iran / Matthew Broyles. —1st ed.
    p. cm.—(Newsmakers)
Includes bibliographical references and index.
ISBN-13: 978-1-4042-1900-7
ISBN-10: 1-4042-1900-5
1. Ahmadinejad, Mahmoud. 2. Presidents--Iran—Biography. 3. Iran--Politics and government—21st century.
I. Title.
DS318.84.A36B76 2008
955.05'44092—dc22
[B]

2007005562

On the cover: Foreground: Iranian president Mahmoud Ahmadinejad. Background: Volunteers of the Islamic Basij militia march outside of Tehran.

CONTENTS

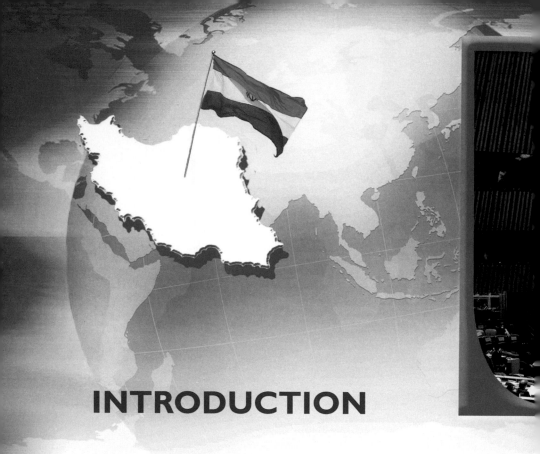

INTRODUCTION

I n September 2006, there was a showdown at the United Nations General Assembly in New York City. From the same podium, within a few hours of each other, U.S. president George W. Bush and Iranian president Mahmoud Ahmadinejad presented the nations of the world with two sides of a disturbing story. That story involved nuclear weapons and the fate of the world.

The United States and Iran had not officially spoken to each other for nearly thirty years, but they had waged a war of words and provided underground support for each other's enemies.

Iranian president Mahmoud Ahmadinejad speaks to the United Nations General Assembly in New York on September 14, 2005, within hours of U.S. president George W. Bush's address from the same podium.

Yet the histories of the United States and Iran are thickly entangled. Iran's pursuit of nuclear technology has once again brought it face to face with the world's largest superpower.

In 2006, Ahmadinejad sent an eighteen-page letter to Bush and later challenged the president to a televised debate. Both of these incidents were ignored by the White House, but since the election of Ahmadinejad to the Iranian presidency in 2005, the United States has found it more difficult to ignore Iran's outspoken new leader.

These sorts of provocative actions are part of Ahmadinejad's dynamic and controversial personality, and they have put him in the spot-light much more than many of his predecessors. He is a man who will plead with Bush and other Western leaders to embrace the kind of the love espoused by Jesus Christ, while at the same time professing hatred for Jews and pledging to destroy Israel.

This book will explore the factors that have made Ahmadinejad who he is, and it will explore the effect he is having on Iran and the Middle East and the possible consequences of his policies around the world.

CHAPTER ONE

PERSIAN AND IRANIAN HISTORY

In order to understand the culture that created Mahmoud Ahmadinejad, it is necessary to review Iran's history, which has been a turbulent one. Iran is home to one of the oldest civilizations in the world. Cyrus the Great, a legendary king, brought the people of the region together into one nation in the sixth century BCE. This nation was called Persia, and under Cyrus and those who came after him, it would become a vast empire. At its most powerful, Persia's borders stretched from India to Turkey to Libya.

CYRUS AND THE PERSIAN EMPIRE

One of the most unusual things about Cyrus's rule is that it set a precedent that has lasted to the present day. While Cyrus conquered some of the nations that became part of the Persian Empire through warfare, most of them were persuaded to yield through negotiation. He was

Macedonia's armies under Alexander the Great defeated the forces of Persian leader Darius III in 333 BCE. Alexander's generals established the Selucid dynasty, which ruled Persia for the next three centuries.

famous for saying that he would only rule as long as his subjects wished it.

The idea that a leader must have the approval of his people in order to rule was drawn from Zoroastrianism, a religion that was founded in ancient Iran and was popular and enduring. Persian rulers were also thought to be intermediaries between God and the people, and their rule was legitimate only if it was just and benefited the best interests of the populace. These same principles would pop up again many times throughout the centuries—long after Zoroastrianism had largely died out—leading to many of the dramatic events in Iran's political history that this book will discuss.

In 333 BCE, the Persian Empire was conquered by Macedonia's Alexander the Great. The empire's splendid capital city, Persepolis, was burned to the ground, and its ruins still lay toppled and uninhabited today.

Though Persia rose again in the third century CE, the empire met a final defeat in 626 CE, at the hands of the Byzantine Empire. But a more important and profound conquering would occur a few decades later. Persia would experience an invasion that would change its culture forever.

THE ARAB INVASION AND CONQUEST

In the seventh century CE, a massive Arab army arose on the windblown desert of the Arabian Peninsula. This army was motivated in large part by a new force in the world: a religion called Islam.

Islam centers on the teachings of Muhammad, who is believed by Muslims to be the chief prophet of God.

Iranians had adjusted to the belief systems of conquerors before, always changing the new, imposed religion around a little to suit their liking. With Islam, this was more difficult, as Iran's new Arab rulers demanded complete conversion. However, an event would soon take place that would provide Iranians with their own perspective on and influence over the Islamic faith.

Zoroastrianism

Zoroastrianism, based on the teachings of the ancient prophet Zoroaster (also known as Zarathustra), was the first religion in the Middle East—and possibly in the world—to worship a single god rather than many gods. It influenced Judaism and, by extension, Christianity and Islam. There are very few Zoroastrians today. However, most of those who still practice the religion continue to live near its birthplace in Iran.

Under Darius I, the Persian Empire grew to its largest size, stretching from Macedonia to Libya to India.

At the time of the Arab conquest of Persia, Muhammad had been dead less than a decade. Soon after Persia's fall to Arabia, there was a great deal of argument and confusion over who was the rightful heir to Muhammad. Violence ensued, and two powerful relatives of Muhammad who were potential successors to him were assassinated—Muhammad's cousin Ali and Ali's son Hussein.

Ali ibn Abi Talib, the prophet Muhammad's cousin and brother-in-law, is shown here. The deaths of Ali and his son Hussein are central events in Shiism.

For a variety of complex reasons, the murders of Ali and Hussein became central events in a new division of Islam called Shiism. Persia, which included modern-day Iran and parts of modern-day Iraq, became the center of this sect, which now accounts for close to 10 percent of the world's Muslim population. The remaining 90 percent are called Sunnis, and they do not attach any special significance to the deaths of Ali and Hussein. But from the time of those murders, Iran once again carved out a unique culture from that imposed by a conquering people. When at last the Arab empire began to fade, Shiism stayed, and it remains the dominant religious, cultural, and political force in Iran to this day.

Arabic rule came to an end in Persia, though Islam took permanent root there. Though the territory that would eventually become known as Iran would be subject to numerous invasions and conquests in the coming centuries, Islam was never displaced by new regimes.

THE SAFAVID DYNASTY

Arab control of Persia yielded to waves of invasions from Turks and Genghis Khan's famously brutal Mongols. The Mongols slaughtered so many people that Iran did not regain its pre-invasion population levels until the twentieth century.

When Mongol power eventually slipped away, a revolutionary dynasty called the Safavids took over. The dynasty was led by a dynamic Shiite warrior named Ismail. Ismail proclaimed himself shah, or king, in 1501, and he immediately declared Shiism the official state religion. Under the Safavids, Persia encompassed most of modern-day Iran and Iraq and expanded its borders once again toward India and Afghanistan.

Shiite and Sunni Muslims

Technically speaking, the difference between Shiite and Sunni beliefs boils down to heredity. Sunnis believe that the first four caliphs (Muhammad's successors) were the true heirs of the Muslim leadership. They believe that caliphs did not need to be descended directly from Muhammad, but could be chosen by tribal consensus. Their view was victorious, as those heirs did rule the vast majority of the Muslim world until the Ottoman Empire's defeat after World War I. Shiites, however, believe that only the heirs of the fourth caliph, Ali, were worthy of leadership.

Since this seemingly simple dispute has been raging for many centuries, numerous other disagreements over doctrine have also broken out, and now there are several ways to distinguish the Shiite and Sunni Islamic faiths. The resulting doctrinal and cultural divide is similar to that existing between Catholic and Protestant Christians, and, as in the dark days of the Protestant Reformation and the Catholic Counter-Reformation, the religious disputes have occasionally led to bloodshed.

Abbas Shah, the most powerful of the Safavids, helped usher in Persia's greatest cultural era, which roughly coincided with the Renaissance in Europe. Persian art and writing reached new heights of beauty and accomplishment during this period. Increased trade around the world brought even more cultural richness to the region.

However, like many powerful leaders through-out Iranian and world history, Abbas was as cruel as he was progressive. Members of his family who might be in a position to challenge his power were blinded and locked away. His iron grip on power would prove to have negative consequences even after he was gone. Following Abbas's death in 1629, the country began to slide into chaos.

THE QAJARS

After a succession of ineffective rulers weakened the country, Persia was overrun by Afghan warriors in 1722. However, these invaders would be thrown out less than a decade later by Nadir Shah, one of the last powerful leaders in Iranian history. Nadir was a Sunni Turk—hardly in tune with the majority of Shiite Persians. But after expelling the Afghans, he mobilized the nation's army to push farther east until they had captured Delhi in India. Nadir's forces looted Delhi, bringing back the jewel-encrusted Peacock Throne, which has been the symbol of Iranian royalty ever since.

Nadir was assassinated in 1747, and chaos reigned until a Turkic tribe called the Qajars took power in 1795. The Qajars would rule Persia until 1925, and their legacy was one of decay and corruption. Their poor management of the country's wealth and natural resources would place Persia at the mercy of opportunistic world powers throughout the twentieth century, setting the stage for the turbulence that now engulfs Iran.

The Qajar shahs were known for lavish spending and luxurious lifestyles. Some of them had harems numbering more than 1,000 women, and they fathered large numbers of princes who spent the nation's wealth with as much abandon as their parents. The shahs kept

Nadir Shah drove the Afghans from Persia and looted the city of Delhi in India, bringing back the famous Peacock Throne.

their vaults full by selling government jobs to the highest bidders, confiscating the fortunes of wealthy merchants, and, most important, selling the country's resources to foreigners.

This last method of raising money would bring about the downfall of the Qajars. Tobacco was a particularly important and valuable domestic commodity that was squandered by the Qajar shahs. In 1891, Nasir al-Din Shah made an agreement with the British Imperial Tobacco Company. The deal required all tobacco grown in Persia to be sold to British Imperial. It also made it illegal to purchase tobacco anywhere in the country from someone other than British Imperial.

RESISTANCE AND REVOLT

As is true throughout Iranian history, religion inspired resistance, change, and revolution. Islamic clerics issued a fatwa, or religious order, declaring that smoking tobacco sold by foreigners was a betrayal of their faith. Across the nation, tobacco sales dropped to nearly zero. Even the shah's many wives received word of the fatwa and stopped smoking altogether. Shocked and bewildered, Nasir al-Din had no choice but to cancel the agreement with British Imperial.

The Persian tradition that leaders could only rule with the consent of their subjects was beginning to reassert itself at the end of the nineteenth century. The people were beginning to recognize that their best interests and those of the nation's were not being served by the corrupt and decadent shahs. This sentiment would only grow as the twentieth century wore on.

In 1901, Muzzaffar al-Din Shah emulated his predecessor's tobacco policy and sold all Iranian petroleum rights to a British merchant named

William Knox D'Arcy. However, it would be many years before D'Arcy would actually strike oil, so, for the time being, the Persian people remained quiet on the issue of signing away the nation's natural resources to foreigners.

The people did not remain quiet at all in December 1905, when a group of merchants were arrested in Tehran, the Persian capital, in a dispute over the price of sugar. The merchants were jailed and tortured by being thrashed on the soles of their feet, a common Qajar punishment.

In the years since the Tobacco Revolt, Persians had made talk of revolution commonplace, whether the radical talk took place at work or around the dinner table. The early twentieth century was characterized by revolutions occurring across the globe, from South Africa to Russia, and stories of underground movements for regime change were filtering in from everywhere. Revolution was ready to explode in Persia, too, and it wouldn't take much to light the fuse.

The Tehran merchants arrested that December likely didn't realize that in the streets outside their prison a revolution was taking place. Citizens took to the streets in vast numbers, shouting demands and completely immobilizing the capital. As the demonstrations went on, the citizens' demands became greater until, eventually, they called for nothing less than the establishment of a parliament where their concerns could be voiced.

After a great deal of struggle and protest, the Persian people got a parliament, called the Majlis, which met for the first time in 1906. This bloodless protest against, and victory over, the ruling shah became known as the Constitutional Revolution. However, the Majlis soon came into conflict with Mohammed Ali Shah, and much of its power was removed. The Constitutional Revolution appeared to be a failure.

REZA SHAH PAHLAVI

In 1925, a fearsome Persian soldier named Reza Khan was approached by the British government to help it overthrow the last of the Qajars, Sultan Ahmad Shah. The British felt they could manipulate Reza Khan and that he could keep a firmer lid on popular unrest that was disrupting trade policies favorable to Britain. Reza Khan became Reza Shah Pahlavi. A decade later, he gave the country its new name: Iran (named after the Aryan peoples who were among the early inhabitants of the territory). Reza Shah ruled until 1941, when the British replaced him with his son, Mohammad Reza Shah Pahlavi, whom they considered easier to control.

Reza Shah embodied the contradictions that often seemed to define Iranian rulers. He was intensely devoted to making Iran a more prosperous society, but he was also extremely intolerant of those who disagreed with him. His problem-solving approach was anything but subtle. He once visited Hamedan in western Iran, and upon learning of local bakers who were hoarding wheat to drive bread prices up, he decided to take action. The first baker he saw was thrown into an oven and burned alive. His approach, though astonishingly cruel, was highly effective. Bread prices went down the very next morning.

Reza Shah Pahlavi, in 1941, abdicates his throne by passing his family's ancestral dagger to his son, Mohammad Reza, who would rule Iran until 1979.

MOHAMMED MOSSADEGH

In the decades since the Constitutional Revolution, something fundamental had changed in Iran. Vast quantities of oil were flowing out of the country, all of it owned by the Anglo-Iranian Oil Company, a British operation that made millions in profits and paid only a tiny portion of those back to

Iran, or rather to the shah. Thousands of
Iranians worked for meager wages to extract
and ship Iran's oil to the rest of the world, and
living conditions were getting worse. The Iranian
people were once again talking of revolution. This
time the spark that lit the fuse of revolution took
the form of an old, frail, but fiery member of the
Majlis: Mohammed Mossadegh.

Mossadegh was one of the most dynamic
figures in Iranian history. Many historians have
argued that if the U.S. Central Intelligence Agency
(CIA) had not eventually carried out a coup to
remove him, the Islamic Revolution, twenty-five
years later, would never have taken place.
Mossadegh was a shrewd politician. Once, on
the floor of the Majlis, he sat silent while Jamal
Emami, a right-wing politician on the British
payroll, railed against him and his criticisms of
the Iranian government. Emami finished by
scornfully saying that if the old man wanted a
real challenge, he should try being prime minister
himself and see how hard the job was. Mossadegh
paused for a moment and then calmly rose to

his feet. He said that he was honored and grateful for the suggestion that he become prime minister and, with great humility, he would be proud to accept. Emami stood stunned as the Majlis erupted in celebration. The motion to make Mossadegh prime minister passed that same day.

Mossadegh's explosive speeches in the Majlis against the Anglo-Iranian Oil Company caught the public's attention and incited their anger. Finally, in 1951, Mossadegh led the Majlis to pass a law removing control of Iran's oil from Anglo-Iranian and placing it in the hands of Iran's new prime minister, who was none other than Mohammed Mossadegh. Public support for this action was so strong and hatred of Anglo-Iranian oil so intense that the politically weakened shah, Mohammad Reza Pahlavi, had no choice but to approve the law. The British embassy was closed, and all British government officials were expelled from the country. The British, needless to say, were furious.

British authorities, left with no influence in Iran, immediately approached the United States for help. President Harry Truman was not

Iran's former prime minister, Mohammed Mossadegh, is shown here while on trial in 1953 for treason. Mossadegh's arrest was orchestrated by the CIA with the shah's cooperation.

receptive, believing that Britain should solve its own problems. At the time, the United States had a good reputation in the region, and Truman sympathized with the nationalist movements to throw off the colonial British yoke in places such as India and Pakistan, for example.

In 1953, using largely false stories of Communist activity within Iran, the British convinced newly elected president Dwight

Eisenhower, a staunch anti-Communist, to come up with a plan to remove Mossadegh from power. This was achieved in a coup staged by the CIA. Mossadegh was imprisoned, the Majlis was weakened, the shah seized more power, and oil revenue was split among a consortium of British and American companies.

The U.S. government did not admit to its role in the coup until 2000, but knowledge of American involvement was widespread in Iran in the years after 1953 and played a large role in the Iranian people's anti-American stance in the years to come. Mohammad Reza Shah Pahlavi only grew more brutal in the wake of the Anglo-Iranian Oil debacle, the foreign meddling in Iran's internal affairs, and the coup. He became determined never to be taken advantage of again, while the people only grew more dissatisfied with his rule.

Just three years after the coup, Mahmoud Ahmadinejad was born.

CHAPTER TWO

AHMADINEJAD AND THE IRANIAN REVOLUTION

Mahmoud Ahmadinejad entered the world on October 28, 1956, in the small village of Garmsar, east of Tehran. Under Mohammad Reza Shah Pahlavi, most industrial jobs had moved to the large cities, impoverishing many small towns, including Garmsar. In his blog, Ahmadinejad describes in somewhat broken English the poverty he was born into:

> [T]he status of the villages became worse than the past. And [for] villagers earning some breadcrumbs, they were deceived by the dazzling look and the misleading features of the cities, and [they] became suburban and lived in ghettos. My family also suffered in the village as others. After my birth—the fourth one in the family— my family was under more pressures. My father had finished [the] sixth grade of

elementary school. He was a hard-bitten
toiler blacksmith, a pious man who regularly
participated in different religious programs.
Even though the dazzling look of the world
was [never] appealing to him, the pressure
of the life [caused him] to migrate to
Tehran when I was one year old. We chose
to live in south central part of Tehran called
Pamenar.

Though he came from modest means, most
of his childhood friends say Ahmadinejad was
extremely bright. Nasir Hadian, who grew up
with him, describes him as the smartest student
in their school. Indeed, Ahmadinejad graduated
at the top of his class in 1976, despite working
in an air-conditioning manufacturer's shop when
his father's income was not enough to support
the family. Ahmadinejad's university entrance
exam scores placed him 132nd among 400,000
who had taken the test that year. He also took
an interest in teaching, tutoring his friends and
neighbors in their homes.

Mohammad Reza Shah Pahlavi is pictured in 1953, the year he temporarily fled Iran under a cloud of public unrest. He would flee again in 1979, never to return.

A POLITICAL AWAKENING

After high school, Ahmadinejad was admitted into Elm Va Sanat University of Tehran as a civil engineering student. While his education was important to him, he was also extremely politically aware. In 1971, while Ahmadinejad was a young student, an event took place that shaped his and most Iranians' view of their government. Mohammad Reza Shah Pahlavi staged a massive celebration of the 2,500th anniversary of the founding of Persia. The event was held among the ruins of Persepolis, the ancient capital, and was one of the most expensive affairs in the history of Iran.

As this lavish and expensive spectacle was held, common people in the surrounding countryside were starving and suffering from a tremendous drought that had shaken Iran that year. What made matters worse was that most Iranians were forbidden to attend the festival at all. Wealthy foreigners from all corners of the globe descended upon Persepolis, partaking of food prepared by 200 chefs flown in from Paris. The

Education in Iran

Iran has a large number of universities. Though they regularly produce students who go on to great success outside the country, these universities are not popular destinations for non-Iranian students because the curriculum is determined by, and steeped in, the Islamic faith. In fact, Iran has had a "brain drain" problem for many years, with its best students migrating to other countries due to a lack of job opportunities within Iran. However, the government still pours a lot of money into its students' education. It is perhaps surprising that in a country where women are denied the many rights and freedoms that are taken for granted by women in the secular (nonreligious) Western world, more women than men are enrolled in Iranian universities.

astonishing banquet featured, among other things, more than one ton of caviar.

Young Ahmadinejad, watching his father struggle to support his family and their meager lifestyle, was appalled to read newspaper reports of the shah's extravaganza. His anger against the government grew, as did that of the majority of Iranian people. This anger was given voice by many prominent Iranians, but no voice was heard more loudly than that of the man who would indirectly shape Ahmadinejad's future and, indeed, all of Iran's: the Ayatollah Khomeini.

AYATOLLAH KHOMEINI AND THE REVOLUTIONARY MOVEMENT

Ruholla Khomeini first appeared on Iran's national stage in 1963, opposing the shah's decision to grant women the right to vote. Khomeini was already a powerful Shiite cleric, but no one knew just how powerful until he was arrested that year on the shah's orders. Massive riots broke out, and hundreds of protesters were killed by police. Eight months later, Khomeini was released, but he continued to agitate against the

Ayatollah Ruholla Khomeini prays with followers in 1978 while exiled in Paris. The next year, he would become Iran's first supreme leader in the wake of the Islamic Revolution.

shah's government. In 1964, he was sent into exile. He would not return for fourteen years, but his influence on Iran's internal affairs would only increase during that period, as he continued to lay the groundwork for revolution.

The revolution Khomeini sought was an Islamic one. He dreamed of establishing a state ruled by Sharia, or Islamic law, as prescribed in the Koran. This was not the goal of many other revolutionary groups in Iran. These ranged from pro-democracy advocates linked to former prime minister Mossadegh to Soviet-backed Communists to more moderate Muslims who wanted some combination of constitutional and Sharia law.

Khomeini knew that his brand of conservative, Islam-based government and society was not everyone's preference. However, he also knew that all of the revolutionary groups shared a hatred of the shah. He believed that, despite their differences, they could accomplish the monarch's overthrow. After overthrowing the shah, they could work out the details of how to rule the nation. Khomeini recorded his pro-Sharia speeches on cassettes and sent them to Iranian mosques. Meanwhile, he spoke in more moderate terms to reporters and leaders of other revolutionary groups. "The religious dignitaries do not want to rule," he assured the Iranian newspaper *Ettelaat* in 1978.

Khomeini's pro-Sharia speeches inspired Ahmadinejad, who spoke about them on his blog years later, again in somewhat broken English:

> Imam [Arabic for "leader"] Khomeini was released from prison. I never forget Imam Khomeini's speeches during those years, which [were] very persuasive and appealing. You would hear the strong faith [in] Almighty God in his orations. He invited the people to pure Islam. His message was [an] invitation to the belief of monotheism—Unity and Oneness of God—and also justice, elimination of oppression, injustice, and sedition in the world. He was courageous and had a valiant heart. He spoke firmly and securely. His orations were simple and honest. The people accepted his guidance sincerely . . . While Imam Khomeini was in exile, I became more familiar with his ideas, thoughts, and philosophy through his companions and disciples in different classes and meetings. The more I became familiar with his thoughts and philosophy, the more affection I had for that divine leader, and his separation and absence [were] intolerable for me.

GROWING DISSATISFACTION WITH THE SHAH'S REGIME

As Ahmadinejad began college, the political situation in Iran grew more unstable. For a start, no one was even sure what year it was. In his drive to Westernize the country, the shah changed the first year of the Iranian calendar from the traditional Islamic *hijri* (the year the prophet Muhammad emigrated from Mecca to Medina) to the ascension of Cyrus the Great to the Persian throne. Suddenly, the current year (1976 in the Western world) was not 1355, but 2535. This enraged many Muslims and strengthened the impression that the shah was out of touch with his subjects. It also seemed to confirm the widespread suspicion that the shah was conducting a cultural war against Islam. This belief would lead to the radicalization of many moderate Muslims.

The Iranian economy was also suffering. The transition from a rural to an industrial economy had taken place in little over a generation and was still shaky. The country's main industry was still oil, and prices in the world oil market were extremely volatile, leading to fluctuating prices within the country as well. This made for an uneasy daily life for the average Iranian and led many to believe that the shah's much-touted Westernization might not be the best option for Iran after all.

The following year brought a glimmer of hope for Iranians suffering under the shah's repressive regime. This hope took the form of newly elected U.S. president Jimmy Carter. Partially to improve the United States' reputation after the end of the Vietnam War, Carter established an Office of Human Rights, which in 1977 began to pressure the shah to improve conditions in his country. The shah was apparently receptive. Soon, certain opposition groups were allowed to demonstrate without the usual brutal police intervention. However, it was too little too late.

That same year, Khomeini's son Mostafa died. Though the autopsy claimed the cause of death was a heart attack, many Muslims were certain that he had been poisoned by the SAVAK, the shah's fearsome secret police force. Sympathy for Khomeini rose, as did his profile in Iran. When the state press ran an article in January 1978 attacking Khomeini, protests broke out in the heavily Shiite holy city of Qom. The police intervened and killed a large number of students, possibly as many as seventy-six. Mosques across the country called on Muslims to honor the dead students in anti-shah protests, which in turn ended with several hundred more deaths at the hands of the police. The cycle of revolutionary violence had begun.

Students were in fact one of the main targets of Khomeini's recruiting efforts for his planned Islamic revolution. His message reached many, including Mahmoud Ahmadinejad. There is no evidence that suggests that Ahmadinejad played a key role in any of the student demonstrations against the government. But his recollections of the era make it clear that he was sympathetic to their cause. In his blog, he writes:

> Even though the revolution was taking place, and I was involved in certain activities against the illegitimate regime of the monarch in

Iran—the mercenary & puppet of U.S. & Britain—I was aware of my education and did not give it up.

Some of Ahmadinejad's cousins have suggested that he may have traveled to Lebanon to help Shiite military forces during the Lebanese civil war, just prior to the revolution, but this cannot be verified.

THE OVERTHROW OF THE SHAH

As 1978 wore on, each new public protest ended more violently than the one before it. Having faced revolution before in 1953, the shah turned once again to his American allies for help. President Carter, however, proved to be less interested in meddling in Iranian internal affairs than was President Eisenhower twenty-five years earlier during the Mossadegh coup. Carter's support only went as far as sending the aircraft carrier USS *Constellation* to the nearby Indian Ocean. Secretly, however, Carter arranged a deal with several Iranian generals to shift their support to a more moderate

Mohammad Reza Shah Pahlavi in January 1979, shakes hands with newly appointed Iranian prime minister Shapour Bakhtiar. The shah would be forced out of Iran forever only days later.

government than that of the shah's. As it turned out, a moderate government would not be on the horizon.

In September 1978, the shah declared martial law, banning all demonstrations. This was a futile move, and protests continued to grow in size. A general labor strike was called in October, grinding major Iranian industry to a halt. The following December happened to be the holy month of Muharram, one of the most important months in the religious calendar for Shiites. On December 12, more than two million people gathered in Tehran to demand the shah's departure. Calls for the return from exile of Khomeini filled the streets.

The last shah of the Pahlavi dynasty was left with no choice. On January 16, 1979, he and his wife left Iran, never to return again. Less than a month later, on February 1, Ayatollah Ruhollah Khomeini returned to Iran, greeted in Tehran by a thunderously loud audience of several million people. Khomeini had returned at the request of the Majlis' prime minister Shapour Bakhtiar, who for the moment seemed to be in charge.

KHOMEINI'S ISLAMIC EXTREMISM

Bakhtiar wanted Khomeini to set up a small religious state in Qom, and he called for the preservation and strengthening of the democratic Iranian constitution. However, Khomeini simply appointed his own prime minister, Mehdi

Bazargan, and declared that "since I have appointed him, he must be obeyed." Disobedience against Khomeini's authority would be regarded as a "revolt against God," as quoted in Baqer Moin's book *Khomeni.*

This sort of talk made many of Khomeini's nonreligious revolutionary allies nervous, and for the next year, the various groups struggled for power. But Khomeini's hold on the Iranian public and his network of Shiite support organizations proved too strong to overcome. In December 1979, the new Iranian constitution proclaimed Khomeini "Supreme Spiritual Leader," a post he would occupy until his death in 1989.

Nineteen seventy-nine would prove to be a pivotal year for the United States as well as Iran. With the fall of the shah, the United States had lost one of its best, most staunch allies in the Middle East. The shah had been reliably pro-American, even though the Iranian people's memory of the 1953 CIA coup against Mossadegh had resulted in widespread hatred for the United States. In a famous speech, Khomeini labeled the

United States the "Great Satan," a name which is still used often in Iran to describe the country.

THE HOSTAGE CRISIS

This hatred overflowed when in October 1979, President Carter allowed the shah asylum in the United States for cancer treatment. On November 4, a group of Iranian students backed by Khomeini took over the U.S. embassy in Tehran, capturing sixty-six Americans who were stationed there. The students pledged to hold the hostages until the shah was returned to Iran for a trial. Many believed that the United States was plotting another coup to reinstall the shah, though Carter was considering no such thing. He did attempt a military rescue mission, Operation Eagle Claw, which failed miserably and resulted in the deaths of eight U.S. soldiers.

The military operation to save the hostages held in the embassy was an undeniable failure. Three of the eight helicopters involved in the mission malfunctioned, and one collided with another support aircraft, killing eight soldiers.

The soldiers' bodies were not retrieved by U.S. forces; instead, they were paraded around on Iranian television for all of the world to see. U.S. secretary of state Cyrus Vance, who had opposed the mission from the beginning, resigned in protest. The Carter administration now had less leverage, and America's reputation suffered, particularly since the crisis came so soon after the country's humiliating withdrawal from Vietnam in 1975.

AHMADINEJAD'S ROLE IN THE HOSTAGE CRISIS?

Recently, there has been some debate over whether Ahmadinejad was among the hostage-taking students. Several former hostages have said that they are certain they recognize him as one of their captors, but many of the known kidnappers deny that he was one of them. Ahmadinejad denies it as well, and no one has been able to prove otherwise.

Ahmadinejad did, however, join a political organization called the Office of Strengthening

Former hostages return to the United States in 1981, after 444 days of captivity in Iran. The hostage crisis was a defining event in U.S.-Iran relations, and it heavily influenced the 1980 U.S. presidential elections.

Unity, or OSU, in 1979. This was a group linked to the hostage takers. It is unclear what his activities in the OSU were during this period.

The American hostages were held for 444 days. They were finally released on January 20, 1981. This also happened to be the day that the new U.S. president, Ronald Reagan, took office. There is a widespread theory in the United States and elsewhere that Ronald Reagan, while still a candidate for the presidency, negotiated a deal with Iran to extend the hostage crisis through the election to make Jimmy Carter look bad. In exchange, the United States would supply Iran with weapons once Reagan took office.

Indeed, the United States did later supply weapons to Iran via the CIA, leading to the Iran-Contra investigations during the Reagan administration. However, the arms sales were never proven to be connected to the Iran hostage crisis.

Reagan defeated Carter in the 1980 election, and many historians have cited Carter's inability to free the hostages as a major factor in his electoral loss. Ahmadinejad's political future, on the other hand, was just getting started.

CHAPTER THREE

THE IRAN-IRAQ WAR

While the United States did not sponsor an Iranian coup in the wake of the Islamic Revolution, it did take sides in a war that broke out shortly after Ayatollah Khomeini took charge of Iran. On September 22, 1980, Iraqi president Saddam Hussein launched an invasion of Iran. The countries had fought before, but the scale of this conflict was much larger. Hussein believed that since Iran was only just emerging from revolution, it would not be organized enough to fend off his military, which at the time was one of the largest and most technologically sophisticated in the Middle East. He had ambitions of controlling as much oil and territory in the region as possible, and he dreamed of building Baghdad into the capital of a new Arab empire.

What Hussein underestimated was the religious fervor of the Iranian people. (Hussein was

Fourteen-year-old Iranian soldiers are held at an Iraqi prisoner-of-war camp in 1988. Young Iranian men were recruited by the thousands to fight in the long and bloody Iran-Iraq War.

himself a Sunni Muslim, but a mostly secular one.) Martyrdom, or death in battle or on behalf of one's religion, is considered to be one of the highest honors in Islam, and Khomeini wasted no time in gathering up vast numbers of young men willing to die fighting the Iraqis. Hussein's army, though technically superior, simply couldn't counter the seemingly inexhaustible supply of zealous (religiously passionate and fanatical) Iranian foot soldiers willing to march to the front lines and resist Hussein's efforts at invasion and domination.

The Iraqi invasion served to unite the people of Iran behind Khomeini. Whatever problems Iranians may have had with his regime, they despised Hussein even more and recognized his threat to their country.

Iranian Soldier-Martyrs

During the Iran-Iraq War, Iranian boys as young as twelve years old would be given small plastic keys that they were told were keys to Paradise. These were given to them under the Khomeini-backed movement Basij, which was primarily aimed at poor communities. Its purpose was to recruit young men to serve on the front lines in the war. However, what these young conscripts were mostly used for was clearing minefields. After being given feverish sermons on the value of martyrdom, the young men would be sent out into minefields, where they were killed or maimed by the thousands.

AHMADINEJAD'S VIEW OF THE WAR

Already loyal to Khomeini, the onset of war inspired Ahmadinejad to join the Revolutionary Guards, also known as the Pasdaran. The Revolutionary Guards are one of the most powerful and least understood of the divisions within the Iranian government. Ahmadinejad thrived in the Guards, becoming a senior officer in their special operations brigade. His specific activities during this period remain classified, as do most Revolutionary Guard records.

The war would grind on for eight more years, killing at least one million people and weakening the economies of both Iran and Iraq. Iraq accepted weapons and money from many Arab and European nations, as well as China and the United States. However, as discussed earlier, Iran was also secretly receiving weapons from the United States, though the amount of U.S. aid to Iraq was considerably larger. The Iranian people knew about the aid to Iraq, and it increased their hatred of the United States. In his blog,

Ahmadinejad recalls the war with Iraq and his disgust with the support that Western nations provided Hussein, support that resulted in the deaths of many innocent Iranian civilians:

> *Saddam, intoxicated with power and receiving all the economic, military, and intelligence support that USA and other Western countries provided him, proudly announced that he will capture Tehran within three days. The war that was imposed on Iran continued for more than eight years instead of three days and, in the end, not even an inch of Iranian land reached the hands of Saddam and his supporters. During these eight years, Saddam fought with us and also with his own people. He bombarded our cities with chemical weapons provided by the Western powers and also Iraqi villages and towns.*

At last, in 1988, the United Nations called for a cease-fire, which finally took hold in August of that year, though the final prisoners of war would

Men in Tehran mourn during the funeral of Ayatollah Khomeini in 1989. The event was chaotic and resulted in Khomeini's body being thrown from his casket by overzealous followers.

not be exchanged between the two countries until 2003. The following year, 1989, saw the death of Khomeini. In his place, the special Assembly of Experts, a group of clerics loyal to Khomeini, selected Seyyed Ali Hossayni Khamenei as the new Supreme Spiritual Leader of Iran, a post he still holds.

POST-WAR OPPORTUNITIES FOR AHMADINEJAD

The end of the Iran-Iraq War brought new opportunities for Ahmadinejad. His service to the government was rewarded with a number of administrative jobs in various Iranian provinces. In 1993, he was appointed governor-general of a newly formed province called Ardabil. In 1997, he received his Ph.D. in traffic and transportation engineering and became a professor at the Iran University of Science and Technology.

Khomeini's Funeral

Ayatollah Khomeini inspired devotion in his followers, but no one was prepared for the chaos that ensued during his 1989 funeral. Mourners, desperate to touch their leader's body one last time, stormed the small wooden casket, at one point knocking Khomeini's body to the ground. The Iranian government was forced to cancel the funeral and hold another one shortly thereafter. This time, the body was encased in a protective steel casket.

The next six years of Ahmadinejad's life would be relatively uneventful. His ambitions were not yet fulfilled. He cofounded the Alliance of Builders of Islamic Iran, or Abadgaran, an extremely conservative political group supported by Khamenei and other conservative clerics. This group began obtaining local and national offices. In the election of 2004, Abadgaran candidates captured almost all of the seats in the Majlis.

A REFORMIST PRESIDENT IS SWORN IN

In 1997, another news-making Iranian, Mohammad Khatami, was sworn in as president of Iran. He became known for introducing liberal-minded, reformist legislation that was frequently opposed by Khamenei and the conservative religious authorities.

These included proposals for more freedom of the press, greater freedoms for women, and less confrontational relations with Western democracies. Most of his proposals were vetoed by Khamenei, but his subsequent landslide re-election in 2001 showed international observers

Former Iranian president Mohammad Khatami speaks in Tehran at a rally in 2001 celebrating the twenty-second anniversary of the Islamic Revolution.

that there was clearly a desire among the Iranian people for a change in their government. How such a change would ever take place is still something of a mystery, given the veto power of the Supreme Spiritual Leader. At any rate, Mahmoud Ahmadinejad would soon be in a position to have his own say in the country's apparent swing toward reform and liberalization.

CHAPTER FOUR

THE IRANIAN SYSTEM OF GOVERNMENT

The organization of Iran's government is unique and, at times, confusing. What follows is a description of the government's arrangement under the 1979 constitution.

SUPREME LEADER

The title of the Supreme Leader, or Supreme Spiritual Leader, is accurate. No decision made by any other branch of government is beyond the Supreme Leader's veto power, with the exception of the Assembly of Experts. The Supreme Leader is commander in chief of the armed forces, and he has the sole ability to declare war. He is responsible for appointing heads of the judiciary, the heads of state radio and television networks, police chiefs, high-ranking military officers, and six of the twelve members of the Council of Guardians. The Supreme Leader can only be selected or dismissed by the Assembly of Experts.

Supreme Spiritual Leader Ayatollah Khamenei of Iran commemorates the sixteenth anniversary of the death of his predecessor, Ayatollah Khomeini, in 2005.

PRESIDENT

The president is elected every four years by popular vote among Iran's citizens. However, a candidate must be approved by the Council of Guardians before he will be allowed to run for office. He is the most powerful individual in the country next to the Supreme Leader. He is technically empowered to exercise executive powers, but all of his decisions can be overruled by the Supreme Leader. He is responsible for appointing the Council of Ministers, officials similar to cabinet members in the United States. The president selects which government policies can be sent to the Majlis for debate and vote. The president does not control the armed forces, but he does appoint the minister of defense. All appointments must be approved by the Majlis.

COUNCIL OF GUARDIANS

The Council of Guardians is made up of twelve members. As mentioned earlier, six are appointed by the Supreme Leader. The other six are recommended by the head of the judiciary (who is also appointed by the Supreme Leader), and they are officially appointed by the Majlis. The council has the authority to veto laws approved by the Majlis if the council determines that they are against Sharia law. The council approves candidates for president and candidates for the Majlis.

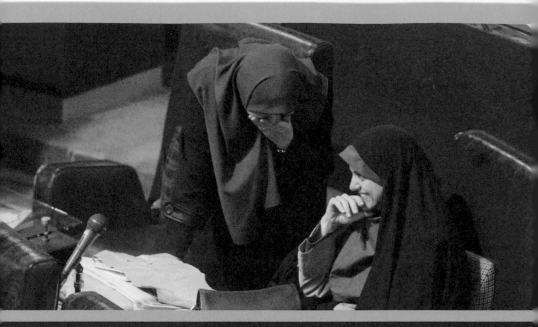

Female reformist representatives attend a 2004 Majlis session. In that year, the Guardian Council refused to let 3,605 reformist candidates run for seats in the Majlis.

EXPEDIENCY COUNCIL

The Expediency Council is charged with handling disputes between the Majlis and the Council of Guardians, and it serves as an advisory board for the Supreme Leader.

MAJLIS

The Majlis is made up of 290 members who are elected in regional elections for four-year terms.

It passes all laws, which must be approved by the Council of Guardians. All Majlis candidates must also be approved by the council.

JUDICIARY

Iran's judicial system is incredibly complex. The type of court an offender will deal with depends entirely upon what kind of crime has been committed. Public courts deal with commonplace crimes, while Revolutionary Courts deal with crimes considered relevant to national security, a category that can be defined broadly. Decisions made by public courts can be appealed, going as far as the Supreme Court, but decisions made by Revolutionary Courts are final.

Still another court, the Special Clerical Court, handles offenses committed by clerics and is accountable only to the Supreme Leader. The head of the judiciary is appointed by the Supreme Leader, and he in turn appoints the head of the Supreme Court and the chief public prosecutor. Analysts familiar with Iran's judicial system say that the court system is actually more complex than the outline given above, but most details of its inner workings and organization are kept classified.

ASSEMBLY OF EXPERTS

The Assembly of Experts meets for one week each year. It is made up of eighty-six members, who are elected by popular vote every eight years. Candidates for the assembly must be approved by the Council of Guardians. The assembly elects the Supreme Leader and can remove him at any time, though it has never done so.

CITY AND VILLAGE COUNCILS

City and village councils are a new development in Iran. They were provided for in the 1979 constitution, but they were not implemented until 1999. Each member of the local councils is elected by a popular vote for a four-year term. The powers of the councils vary depending on the location, but they generally concern themselves with local issues.

This dizzying division of power is often perplexing, and it is often not adhered to closely.

Iranians cast their votes in the 2006 election for local councils and the Assembly of Experts, the year after Ahmadinejad became president.

In 2006, ABC News reporter and *Nightline* anchor Ted Koppel recounted his difficulty in finding out who was in charge in one of Iran's provinces, while speaking to a local governor-general:

> *I say, do you mean the Revolutionary Guard?*
> *And he says, yeah, but the faceless ones. And*
> *I said, well, you mean the intelligence branch*

of the Revolutionary Guard? And he says yes. And then he says, but they're talking to a guy whom we somewhat disrespectfully referred to as the fat guy because none of us could remember his name. And it turned out that the fat guy had a great deal of influence with the local branch of Hezbollah. Now, this is in Iran, right on the border with Iraq. And I ended up interviewing him, and he turned out to be a very well-informed man. And at the end of the interview, I said, look, I under-stand you have a great deal of contact with Hezbollah. Can you set me up to talk to some of the guys with Hezbollah? And he said, no, but you've already talked to the head of Hezbollah because I am the head of Hezbollah in this region. So, one of the interesting things about Iran is it's always difficult to know who is really running the show in different sections of town. There are places where having a permit from the central government is absolutely and totally meaningless. The local folks couldn't care less.

THE STALLING OF REFORM

As complicated as Iran's authority structure can be, the president is certainly the one leader most familiar to people outside of Iran. He is the most visible leading official in Iran, holding press conferences, attending UN sessions, and hosting visiting diplomats. The president sets the tone for what the rest of the world thinks about Iran.

For this reason, it was big news when a reformer such as Khatami was twice elected to Iran's second-highest office. It was seen as a sign that Iran might be on the verge of softening the hard-line domestic and political positions it had advocated since the 1979 revolution. However, one look at this complex governmental structure reveals just how little effect an Iranian president can have on the course his country takes. For a start, for him to be approved to run at all, he must have the blessing of the Council of Guardians, which in turn must have the blessing of the Supreme Leader. Since both the Guardians and the Supreme Leader tend to be conservative

Islamists, any candidate touted as a "reformer" is likely to be able to operate only within a narrow range of policy. An Iranian president is unlikely to be able to usher in any sweeping social, religious, cultural, or political changes that are out of step with conservative Islamic law and culture.

Following the terms of two reformist presidents—Khatami and his predecessor, Akbar Hashemi Rafsanjani—whose attempts at reform had mostly come to nothing, a new star was rising in Iran. Mahmoud Ahmadinejad's time had come.

CHAPTER FIVE

AHMADINEJAD RISES TO POWER

In 2003, Mahmoud Ahmadinejad ran for a seat on Tehran's fifteen-member city council. Only 12 percent of the city's population had turned out to vote, and the majority of those were hard-line conservatives mobilized by groups such as the Alliance of Builders of Islamic Iran. The newly elected council appointed Ahmadinejad mayor of Tehran, and he wasted no time in advancing his agenda.

FRIEND TO THE POOR

Ahmadinejad spoke a lot about his background as a poor blacksmith's son, and he spent a great deal of time promoting projects to improve the lives of the poor and downtrodden. He diverted funds to many public works projects, including a subway system for traffic-heavy Tehran. He made shows of solidarity with low-income workers such as street sweepers. Ahmadinejad

An Iranian man sells flowers on the street. Iran has a high unemployment rate, and its citizens have to find whatever means they can of making a living.

even continued to live in a modest house in the low-income suburban neighborhood where he grew up.

Ahmadinejad established his conservative political and religious credentials, promoting a strict brand of Islam that harkened back to the days of Ayatollah Khomeini, a man whom he still idolized. He found a warm and welcoming audience among Tehran's poor residents, many of whom fondly remembered Khomeini's speeches in support of lifting up the nation's poor. Ahmadinejad invoked the 1979 revolution often, setting him apart from other politicians who garnered votes by trying to relax the more strict policies of the post-revolution era.

Ahmadinejad began to gain many admirers, but he also attracted some critics. President Khatami refused to allow Ahmadinejad to attend cabinet meetings, while previous Tehran mayors had always been welcome. Many upper-class Iranians derided him as a "village idiot" for his simple arguments on behalf of the nation's poor. But it was just these simple, uncomplicated arguments that brought him in line with fans of Khomeini, who would prove useful to him in the near future.

ENTERING THE PRESIDENTIAL RACE

Ahmadinejad was scarcely into his second year as mayor of Tehran before he entered the 2005 Iranian presidential election. Press within and outside of Iran didn't take a great deal of notice of the largely unknown candidate, particularly since the front-runner was former President Rafsanjani, who was expected to win relatively easily. However, Rafsanjani's campaigning centered mostly on urban areas—Tehran, in particular— where his usual reform-minded base lived. Ahmadinejad spent weeks on the road in far-flung rural provinces, gathering support from poor communities who took comfort in his message of economic improvement. "He looks like us and talks like us. And he promised to look out for us, something that no other politician has done," Ghaffar Jalilvand, a shopkeeper from Takestan, a small town far from Iran's capital city, told *Washington Post* reporter Karl Vick.

With his base in the impoverished Tehran neighborhoods, enough votes were cast for Ahmadinejad that a runoff was required between himself and Rafsanjani. The former president had won the most votes, but not enough to constitute a clear majority.

In the lead-up to the runoff, Iranian voters learned more about this little-known politician and his championing of traditional revolutionary

Ahmadinejad waits in line to cast his ballot during the 2005 runoff election between himself and former president Rafsanjani. Though standing in line with ordinary Iranians, he is surrounded by bodyguards.

values. One voter, Rohollah Samimi, made this point to Vick: "The people actually did test the reformists during the last eight years, but they didn't see much from them. So people here decided to return to the people who are promoting revolutionary values and see if they can bring about change."

During the runoff, the people of Iran also got to see more of Ahmadinejad's personality.

Even Ahmadinejad's enemies have commented on his charisma and the certainty of his beliefs. This proved attractive to many Iranians, and he won the runoff election, defeating Rafsanjani in a landslide. Rafsanjani was philosophical about the possibility of an Ahmadinejad presidency: "If my rival wins, I don't think it will create problems for the country because I will be on the scene and defend our revolution and our country" (as quoted in Vick's *Washington Post* article).

This was not mere talk, for Rafsanjani headed the Expediency Council, which always has the ear of the Supreme Leader.

MAKING ENEMIES WITH INFLAMMATORY WORDS

The reaction of governments around the world to Ahmadinejad's election was nothing short of pandemonium. Though Ahmadinejad was the first post-revolutionary Iranian president who was not also a cleric, his words echoed those of Ayatollah Khomeini more than any Iranian president in recent memory. "My mission is creating a role model of a modern, advanced, powerful, and Islamic society," Ahmadinejad said in accepting his victory (as quoted by Margaret Coker in an article for *Cox Newspapers*).

A fiery speech at the UN General Assembly in September 2005 further stoked Western nations' fear of an Ahmadinejad regime. The United States was particularly concerned. While pleading with God to bring about the Twelfth Imam (Shiite Islam's Messiah figure), he spoke of Iran's controversial nuclear program. He added this warning: "If some try to impose their will on the Iranian people through resort to a language of force and threat with Iran, we will reconsider our entire approach to the nuclear issue" (as quoted in a *Washington Post* article by Dafna Linzer).

More disturbing to outside observers was Ahmadinejad's recollection of the speech afterward. He claimed that as he was speaking, a light surrounded him. "All of a sudden, the atmosphere changed. For twenty-seven minutes, the leaders did not blink. They were astonished

Ahmadinejad speaks at a general debate at the United Nations three days after his controversial address to the UN General Assembly.

as if a hand held them there and made them sit. It had opened their eyes and ears for the message of the Islamic Republic" (as quoted in Bob Woodruff's profile for ABC News).

The idea that a country with a leader who claimed to be subject to mystical visions might soon obtain nuclear weapons put a chill down the spines of Western leaders. Interestingly, it also alarmed many Iranian clerics. "If he really did say this, then it is certainly wrong, and it is certainly treason," said Grand Ayatollah Yusef Saanei (as quoted by Woodruff). But other Iranians were glad to have a leader who caught the world's attention. "He may look ridiculous in your eyes. He sometimes looks ridiculous in our eyes. But he stands up for the nation," Manesh Ganji, a civil engineer living in Tehran, told Margaret Coker. "When he speaks, the world listens."

Indeed, the world did listen. U.S. president George W. Bush (who had already labeled Iran part of the "Axis of Evil," along with Iraq and North Korea) was listening very closely. Bush immediately pressed the United Nations to step up its efforts in halting the Iranian nuclear program.

Ahmadinejad, however, was not finished alarming the West. Only a month after his UN speech, he made a comment concerning Israel, the Jewish nation that the United States considers its closest Middle Eastern ally. He quoted and agreed with Khomeini's statement that Israel should be eliminated from the pages of history. Inflammatory as these words were, the phrase "eliminated from the pages of history" was mistranslated in the media as "wiped off the map." Fury erupted in the Israeli and American press, and Ahmadinejad

The United Nations Security Council

Originally conceived as an international guardian of peace and security after the devastation of World War II, the United Nations has evolved into an extremely controversial organization since its founding in 1945. Ahmadinejad and other world leaders have attacked the structure of the Security Council, which has five permanent, unchanging members (China, France, the United States, England, and the Russian Federation), each with the power to veto any decision made by the council. Many UN critics, including well-known political theorist Noam Chomsky, believe that this makes the council biased against smaller countries whose interests may be different than those of the nations with veto power.

Protesters demonstrate outside the Iran vs. Portugal World Cup soccer match in Frankfurt, Germany, in 2006. The cartoon posters reflect anger at Ahmadinejad's comments regarding Israel's right to exist.

was seen more and more as an anti-Semitic madman who must not be allowed the keys to nuclear technology.

Ahmadinejad still wasn't finished. Two months later, he gave a speech in which he denied that the Holocaust, in which six million Jews died at the hands of the German Nazi regime, had ever taken place. He claimed to a crowd of supporters in Iran that Jews had invented the Holocaust as a myth, one that gave them power over other people and religions.

When asked in interviews about his Holocaust comments, Ahmadinejad redirected the question, asking why Palestinians, who had no role in the "alleged" Holocaust, should have to give up their land to accommodate displaced Jews, an argument that has been made by others as well. Pressed further on why he believed the Holocaust was a myth, Ahmadinejad called for investigations by European authorities into the truth of the events, upon which no reputable historian casts doubt.

After only a few months in office, Ahmadinejad had renewed Iran's reputation for annoying, frustrating, and frightening the West. The negotiation process over Iran's nuclear capability was going to be rocky indeed.

CHAPTER SIX

AHMADINEJAD AND IRAN'S NUCLEAR PROGRAM

Iran's nuclear program was a source of worry for the United Nations even before Ahmadinejad took office. In August 2002, Iranian exiles reported that the government had built a uranium enrichment plant and a heavy water plant, two elements essential for nuclear energy production. They had done so without informing the International Atomic Energy Authority (IAEA), a nuclear enforcement arm of the United Nations. Later that year, U.S. satellite photographs confirmed the existence of the reported sites. Iran admitted that it was pursuing nuclear energy, but insisted it was only for peaceful purposes. The IAEA convinced Iran to prove its intentions by submitting to inspections of its nuclear facilities.

A. Q. KHAN AND THE SELLING OF NUCLEAR SECRETS

In August 2003, inspections found traces of highly enriched weapons-grade uranium at the

The chief architect of Pakistan's nuclear weapons program, Dr. A.Q. Khan, is shown in a 2004 photo. Khan has admitted giving nuclear technology secrets to Iran.

nuclear sites. Iran agreed to a tougher round of inspections. However, in February 2004, revelations emerged about a connection between Iran and the man known as the father of Pakistan's nuclear weapons program, Abdul Qadeer (A. Q.) Khan. Khan gave a televised confession, admitting that he passed nuclear secrets to Iran, as well as to North Korea and Libya.

Hated and feared by Western governments, the man who brought Pakistan the atomic bomb is regarded as a hero in much of the Muslim world. Khan was a member of a Dutch nuclear energy team in the early 1970s, and after India tested its first nuclear bomb, he began passing secret nuclear technology to the nervous Pakistani government, who expected to be the intended target of India's new weapons. In 1976, he went to work directly for the Pakistani government. In 1987, he announced that Pakistan had achieved nuclear weapons capability, the first Islamic nation to do so. This would have frightened the West enough, but during the 1990s, Khan began selling nuclear secrets to other nations despised by the United States and its allies, including Iran, North Korea, and Libya. In the wake of overwhelming evidence, Pakistan made a show of removing Khan from his job as punishment for this action, but Pakistani president General Pervez Musharraf pardoned him shortly thereafter.

SHOWDOWN WITH THE WEST

Shortly after this revelation, Iran agreed to suspend uranium enrichment, but evidence uncovered by further inspections showed that it had not done so. In September 2004, U.S. secretary of state Colin Powell called for UN Security Council sanctions against Iran. Iran agreed to hold talks with the European Union

Secretary General Kofi Annan of the UN greets Iranian diplomats in New York during negotiations over Iran's nuclear program.

instead to discuss incentives for halting its nuclear program. The EU held firm to its stance that the Iranian situation could be handled by negotiation rather than sanctions.

The standoff between the United States, the EU, and Iran escalated for the next year, until at last the dam broke in August 2005: Mahmoud Ahmadinejad was elected the president of Iran.

Now the United States was having none of the European Union's talk of negotiation, and it began to press harder for sanctions. Though the United States has toughened its stance since 2005, and though all other permanent members of the Security Council have publicly agreed that sanctions are appropriate, no sanctions have been applied to Iran at the time of this writing.

The reasons for this can be speculated upon endlessly. The presence of U.S. troops on Iran's western border with Iraq and on its eastern border with Afghanistan would seem to give the United States some bargaining power. But the deterioration of conditions within those two countries and the overwhelming military challenges that such a situation requires seem to have emboldened Ahmadinejad. He has ignored American threats. Indeed, his attitude toward the U.S. government has scarcely changed as the crisis has escalated. In September 2006, he suggested that since Bush was demanding that Iran forego its nuclear ambitions, the United States should also be required to shut down its own nuclear program. In addition, he made the audacious claim that in five years, Iran would sell its fuel to the United States at a 50 percent discount.

The bargaining stance of the United States seems to have become so dire that for the first time since the 1979 hostage crisis, its government is hinting at the possibility of direct talks with Iran. Supreme Leader Ali Khamenei has publicly brushed aside any idea of such talks taking place, but Ahmadinejad has suggested that talks might be considered if sanctions were taken off the table at the Security Council. As has always been the case with Iranian politics, it is difficult to know whom to listen to and who has the most leverage and the real decision-making authority.

AHMADINEJAD ADDRESSES AMERICANS DIRECTLY

President Ahmadinejad remains Iran's major mouthpiece as far as the rest of the world is concerned. In November 2006, he took the unusual step of publishing an open letter not to the American government, but to its people. The letter was posted shortly after the 2006 midterm congressional elections, in which the Democratic Party, President Bush's chief domestic rivals, had retaken the majority in both houses. Ahmadinejad addresses this specifically in his open letter to the American people:

> *The legitimacy, power, and influence of a government do not emanate from its arsenals of tanks, fighter aircrafts, missiles, or nuclear weapons. Legitimacy and influence reside in sound logic, quest for justice, and compassion and empathy for all humanity. The global position of the United States is in all probability weakened because the administration has continued to resort to force, to conceal the truth, and to mislead the American people about its policies and practices. Undoubtedly, the American people are not satisfied with this behavior and they showed their discontent in the recent elections. I hope that in the wake of the mid-term elections,*

the administration of President Bush will have heard and will heed the message of the American people."

This approach of bypassing politicians and directly addressing a nation's people is similar to the one taken by Bush, who has repeatedly appealed to the people of Iran to set their government on a more peaceful course.

Though many Americans consider Ahmadinejad crazy, he is also undeniably savvy. He knows how to exploit Americans' growing weariness with a seemingly endless, unwinnable war and concerns about the resulting fraying of the American social fabric. "I think that Mr. Bush can be in the service of his own people," Ahmadinejad said in a 2006 interview with CBS's Mike Wallace. "He can save the American economy [by] using appropriate methodologies without killing people, innocents, without occupation, without threats. I am very saddened to hear that I percent of the total [U.S.] population is in prison. And 45 million people don't have health-care [coverage]. That is very sad to hear."

MIXED OPINIONS ABOUT AHMADINEJAD

Within Iran, opinions about the outspoken president are mixed. Opponents such as Rafsanjani say that Ahmadinejad's confrontational style has given the United States ammunition to convince other nations of Iran's threat to world peace. Sayeed Jazy, a childhood friend of Ahmadinejad's, has a different perspective. He believes that the president likes to put on a good show to get what he wants. Addressing Ahmadinejad's comment about removing Israel from the pages of history, he says, "You sit down and ask him, 'Do you really want to do that?' He would say no. Because I know him, he's not like that. No one in their right mind would accept that" (as quoted by Woodruff).

Indeed, Ahmadinejad's hard-line facade does seem to have cracks. He has not strictly enforced Iran's dress code for women, an important part of Sharia law. He recently announced that women would be allowed into sporting events, a forbidden privilege since 1979, only to have his decision overturned by the Supreme Leader in a rare clash between the two.

Nevertheless, Ahmadinejad's reputation for rigid commitment to conservative Islamic values is well-deserved, say other Iranian observers. "He is a believer . . . [in] a clash of civilizations in which Islam is the only credible alternative to Western domination," political analyst Amir Taheri told Margaret Coker, "and he is convinced that Islam will win." Similar things have been said about U.S. president George W. Bush, a conservative Christian, who holds the view that the end of days as prophesied in the Bible are coming sooner rather than later.

IRAN AS REGIONAL POWER BROKER

Conflict in the Middle East is nothing new, but the early years of the twenty-first century mark the first time since World War II that the United States has had so many of its own forces in the eye of the storm. The U.S. military presence in Iran's Islamic neighbors Afghanistan and Iraq has united many Iranians in religious

Iraqis mourn the death of a family member in the city of Fallujah during an expansion of Sunni vs. Shiite violence in 2006.

outrage and proud nationalism in much the same way that Saddam Hussein's invasion of Iran did more than twenty years ago.

As discussed earlier, modern-day Iran is not the only home of Shiism. The south of Iraq is home to many of the most important Shiite shrines, and since the fall of Hussein's Sunni-led regime, Shiites have begun to assert their influence in that region. Many U.S. analysts at the beginning of the Iraq War believed that Iraqi Shiites would consider themselves Iraqis first and Shiites second, limiting the amount of leverage that Iran could exert in Iraq. After all, the two nations had fought each other for nearly a decade in one of the bloodiest and most prolonged conflicts of the twentieth century.

This theory has proven to be incorrect thus far. Shiites in both nations are united in their joy that Hussein, the instigator of the horrific Iran-Iraq War, has been removed, and they seem to be taking the opportunity of his absence to grow closer. Iraqi Shiite leaders meet regularly with Iranian government officials. They are often members of the same political organizations. At the time of this writing, the party holding the majority in the Iraqi parliament is the Islamic Dawa Party, a Shiite organization that has operated on both sides of the Iran-Iraq border since the 1950s.

Upon taking office in 2005, Iraq's interim prime minister, Ibrahim al-Jaafari, made a pilgrimage to Iran to visit Ayatollah Khomeini's grave and to meet with his successor, Ali Khamenei. Upon his return, al-Jaafari said Iraq hoped to put the memory of the Iran-Iraq War behind it and forge new ties of brotherhood with Iran.

Ahmadinejad appears to agree with al-Jaafari and has stated many times that Iran has the ability to make things much more difficult in Iraq for the Americans anytime it wishes. Shiite ties between Iran and Iraq are now tight and show no signs of weakening. Shiite militias operating in Iraq might respond to orders received from Tehran to harass and attack U.S. forces in heavily Shiite regions in the nation.

As mentioned earlier, the United States' predicament in Iraq is worsening its predicament with Iran. In late 2006, Bush assigned a special commission, the Baker-Hamilton Iraq Study Group, to come up with possible solutions for the chaotic Iraqi situation. Their recommendations were released in December 2006, and one of them was to open direct talks with Iran. At the time of this writing, it is unclear whether the Bush administration will reverse nearly three

Ahmadinejad speaks at a 2006 conference in Tehran addressing security in neighboring Iraq. In this speech, Ahmadinejad again mentioned regime change in Israel.

decades of U.S. policy and speak directly with the Iranian government. Though Ahmadinejad has offered to engage Bush in discussions, these are hardly the circumstances that American officials would choose in which to hold them.

The situation is made more complicated by the fact that Iran is well-known as a sponsor of terrorist groups such as Hezbollah in Lebanon. From July through August 2006, Hezbollah forces in Lebanon exchanged vicious attacks with Israel across their shared border. More than 1,000 Lebanese and Israeli citizens were killed before a UN cease-fire ended the violence. Iran's role in the attacks is unclear, apart from providing a large amount of the funding and weaponry that Hezbollah relies on.

When asked about the Iranian role in the Hezbollah-Israel conflict, Ahmadinejad turned the tables on CBS's Mike Wallace: "The laser-guided bombs have been given to the Zionists [Israelis], and they're targeting the shelter of defenseless children and women. So we are asking, why the American government is blindly supporting this murderous regime?" This approach to debate is one reason why American officials may not be relishing the idea of face-to-face negotiations with Iran's feisty leader. When Wallace asked him whether he wished to speak with the American government, he cagily replied, "Who cut the relations? I ask you."

Iran is suspected of sponsoring, funding, and possibly orchestrating terrorist activities throughout the Middle East and beyond. The United States has a policy of never negotiating with terrorists and of not distinguishing between the terrorists and those who sponsor them. Therefore, dialogue between the two nations would be difficult, to say the least. They seem to be at an impasse, from which neither side is willing to budge.

The future of the Middle East, and indeed the world, rests at least in part on the West's ability to deal with Ahmadinejad. He is the latest in a long line of unique and controversial Iranian leaders, stretching from Cyrus, Abbas Shah, and Reza Shah to Mossadegh and Ayatollah Khomeini. When the history of the twenty-first century is written, the name Ahmadinejad will undoubtedly be featured prominently.

TIMELINE

1956 October 26, Mahmoud Ahmadinejad is born in Garmsar, Iran.

1976 Ahmadinejad graduates at the top of his high school class and enters Elm Va Sanat University of Tehran.

1979 January 16, Mohammad Reza Shah Pahlavi departs Iran under massive public pressure. Ayatollah Ruholla Khomeini returns to Iran from exile shortly thereafter, and by year's end he establishes the new Islamic republic government.

1979 Ahmadinejad joins the Office of Strengthening Unity, a Khomeini-supported student political organization.

1979 November 4, American hostages taken by OSU-affiliated student group at U.S. embassy.

1980 September 22, Iraqi dictator Saddam Hussein launches Iran-Iraq War, which will continue for eight years.

1980 Ahmadinejad joins Revolutionary Guards, a secretive arm of Khomeini's government.

1981   January 20, American hostages are released.

1988   August, Iran-Iraq War ends. Ahmadinejad begins series of provincial administrative jobs.

1989   June 3, Ayatollah Khomeini dies. Ayatollah Ali Khamenei is designated his successor as Supreme Leader.

1993   Ahmadinejad appointed governor-general of Ardabil province.

1997   Ahmadinejad receives Ph.D. in traffic and transportation engineering. He becomes a professor at the Iran University of Science and Technology.

2003   Ahmadinejad wins Tehran city council seat and is appointed mayor by the council.

2005   Ahmadinejad wins Iranian presidential election, beating favored opponent Akbar Hashemi Rafsanjani.

2005   September, Ahmadinejad speaks forcefully at the UN General Assembly, affirming Iran's right to nuclear technology.

TIMELINE

2005 October, Ahmadinejad quotes Khomeini in reference to Israel's continued existence, affirming the late ayatollah's declaration that the Jewish nation should be "eliminated from the pages of history."

2005 December, Ahmadinejad denies the historical occurrence of the Holocaust.

2006 May 8, Ahmadinejad sends an eighteen-page letter to U.S. president George W. Bush.

2006 November 29, Ahmadinejad writes an open letter to the American people.

2006 December 11, Ahmadinejad convenes an International Conference to Review the Global Vision of the Holocaust. Iranian officials insist the symposium is not meant to disprove the Holocaust's occurrence, though infamous anti-Semitic speakers such as former Ku Klux Klan leader David Duke are invited to speak.

2007 Ahmadinejad states his intention to attend a session of the United Nations Security Council in which member nations are to vote on a resolution that would place additional sanctions on Iran for failing to halt uranium enrichment.

Glossary

ayatollah A religious leader among Shiite
Muslims.

Byzantine Empire The eastern half of the
Roman Empire, which survived for 1,000
years after the western half had crumbled
into various feudal kingdoms. The Byzantine
Empire finally fell to Ottoman Turkish
onslaughts in 1453.

cabinet A group of advisors to a head of state
or other high official.

colonial Relating to the practice of colonialism,
a political-economic phenomenon whereby
various European nations explored, conquered,
settled, and exploited large areas of the
world, including the Middle East.

Communist A person who supports
Communism, a system of political and
economic organization in which property is

owned by the state or community, and all citizens share in the common wealth, more or less according to their need.

consortium An agreement, combination, or group (as of companies) formed to undertake an enterprise that would be beyond the resources of any one member.

coup Short for coup d'etat, a term describing the violent overthrow or alteration of an existing government by a small group of rebels.

drought A period of dryness that causes extensive damage to crops or prevents their successful growth. Due to the damage it causes to agriculture, drought can often lead to famine.

dynasty A powerful group or family that maintains its leadership position for a considerable time.

Genghis Khan Thirteenth-century Mongolian warrior-ruler, one of the most famous conquerors of history, who consolidated tribes into a unified Mongolia and extended his empire across Asia to the Adriatic Sea.

Iran-Contra A 1980s-era scandal involving weapons sold to Iran. The profits from these sales were funneled to the Nicaraguan Contras, a right-wing, anti-Communist rebel militia supported by the United States. This movement of money was illegal under a 1984 law; Senate hearings ensued.

Lebanese Civil War A civil conflict resulting from tensions among Lebanon's Christian and Muslim populations and worsened, in the 1970s, by the presence in Lebanon of fighters from the Palestine Liberation Organization (PLO), an anti-Israeli organization.

martyr A person who voluntarily suffers death as the penalty for defending or refusing to renounce a religion.

Marxist Similar to a Communist, though more devoted to the teachings of Karl Marx, on whose theories much of Communism was founded.

monotheism The belief that there is only one god.

mosque A building used for public worship by Muslims.

nationalist A member of a political party or group advocating national independence or strong national government.

parliament A national legislative body usually charged with debating and passing laws, among other duties. In Iran, the parliament is known as the Majlis.

petroleum An oily, flammable liquid that may vary in color from almost clear to black. It is prepared for use as gasoline, naphtha, or other products that are refined and used as fuel or solvents (cleaning products).

secular Not overtly or specifically religious.

Soviet Union Officially named the Union of Soviet Socialist Republics, this was a Communist nation centered in present-day Russia that existed from 1917 until 1991. After World War II, it was one of two world superpowers, along with the United States. The rivalry between these nations, from 1945 to 1991, was known as the Cold War.

Turks Members of any of numerous Asian peoples speaking Turkic languages who live in a region extending from the Balkans to eastern Siberia and western China.

veto The power of one branch of an organization or government to block an action or law approved by another branch.

Vietnam War A conflict between the Communist government of North Vietnam and its allies in South Vietnam (known as the Vietcong) against the government of South Vietnam and its principal ally, the United States. The war was also part of a larger regional conflict and a manifestation of the Cold War between the United States and the Soviet Union and their respective allies. The United States withdrew from Vietnam in 1975, and the South Vietnamese were defeated shortly thereafter.

Westernize Referring to an effort to introduce political, cultural, and economic elements of the United States and western Europe to Eastern and/or undeveloped, undemocratic nations. Often refers to establishing heavy industry and trading with foreign companies and governments.

For More Information

American-Iranian Council
20 Nassau Street, Suite 111
Princeton, NJ 08542
(609) 252-9099
Web site: http://www.american-iranian.org/

Foundation for the Children of Iran
7201 West 78th Street, Suite 100
Bloomington, MN 55439
(952) 896-9190
Web site: http://www.childrenofiran.org/

Foundation for Democracy in Iran
7831 Woodmont Avenue, Suite 395
Bethesda, MD 20814
(301) 946-2918
Web site: http://www.iran.org/

Foundation for Iranian Studies
4343 Montgomery Avenue
Bethesda, MD 20814
(301) 657-1990
Web site: http://www.fis-iran.org/

Iran Heritage Foundation
5 Stanhope Gate
London, England WIK IAH
Web site: http://www.iranheritage.org/

Iran Society
2 Belgrave Square
London, England SWIX 8PJ
Web site: http://www.iransoc.dircon.co.uk/

Middle East Studies Association
The University of Arizona
1219 N. Santa Rita Avenue
Tucson, AZ 85721
(520) 621-5850
Web site: http://mesa.wns.ccit.arizona.edu/

World Health Organization
Iran WHO Representative Office
P.O. Box 14665-1565
Tehran, Iran
Web site: http://www.who.int/countries/irn/en/

WEB SITES

Due to the changing nature of Internet links, Rosen Publishing has developed an online list of Web sites related to the subject of this book. This site is updated regularly. Please use this link to access the list:

http://www.rosenlinks.com/nm/maah

For Further Reading

Clawson, Patrick, and Michael Rubin. *Eternal Iran: Continuity and Chaos*. New York, NY: Palgrave MacMillan, 2005.

Ebadi, Shirin. *Iran Awakening: A Memoir of Revolution and Hope*. New York, NY: Random House, 2005.

Gheissari, Ali, and Vali Nasr. *Democracy in Iran: History and the Quest for Liberty*. New York, NY: Oxford University Press, 2006.

Molavi, Afshin. *The Soul of Iran: A Nation's Journey to Freedom*. New York, NY: W. W. Norton, 2005.

Satrapi, Marjane. *Persepolis: The Story of a Childhood*. New York, NY: Pantheon, 2003.

Takeyh, Ray. *Hidden Iran: Paradox and Power in the Islamic Republic*. New York, NY: Times Books, 2006.

Zanganeh, Lila Azam. *My Sister, Guard Your Veil; My Brother, Guard Your Eyes: Uncensored Iranian Voices*. Boston, MA: Beacon Press, 2006.

Bibliography

Ahmadinejad, Mahmoud. Blog. Blog entries retrieved November 2006 (http://www.ahmadinejad.ir/).

Clawson, Patrick, and Michael Rubin. *Eternal Iran: Continuity and Chaos*. New York, NY: Palgrave Macmillan, 2005.

Coker, Margaret. "Ahmadinejad Taps Nationalist Fervor, Savors Role as Firebrand." Cox Newspapers. September 22, 2006. Retrieved November 2006 (http://www.coxwashington. com/news/content/reporters/stories/2006/ 09/22/BC_IRAN_PRESIDENT22_COX.html).

Conan, Neal. "Talk of the Nation" Interview with Ted Koppel. NPR.org. November 16, 2006. Retrieved November 2006 (http:// www.npr.org/templates/transcript/transcript. php?storyId=6497391).

Encyclopedia Brittanica. *Iran: The Essential Guide to a Country on the Brink*. Hoboken, NJ: Wiley, 2006.

Hiro, Dilip. *The Iranian Labyrinth: Journeys Through Theocratic Iran and Its Furies*. New York, NY: Nation Books, 2005.

HNN staff. "What Is The Difference Between Sunni and Shiite Muslims—And Why Does It Matter?" George Mason University's History News Network (HNN). September 9, 2002. Retrieved November 2006 (http://hnn.us/articles/934.html).

"The Hostage Crisis in Iran." Jimmy Carter Library and Museum. February 2006. Retrieved November 2006 (http://www.jimmycarterlibrary.org/documents/hostages.phtml).

"Iranian Leader: Holocaust a 'Myth.'" CNN.com. December 14, 2005. Retrieved November 2006 (http://www.cnn.com/2005/WORLD/meast/12/14/iran.israel/).

Keddie, Nikki R. *Modern Iran: Roots and Results of Revolution*. New Haven, CT: Yale University Press, 2006.

Kinzer, Stephen. *All the Shah's Men: An American Coup and the Roots of Middle East Terror*. Hoboken, NJ: Wiley, 2004.

BIBLIOGRAPHY

Koppel, Ted. "Koppel on Discovery: Iranians
Speak." Discovery Channel. November 2006.
Retrieved November 2006 (http://dsc.
discovery.com/convergence/koppel/iran/
people/people.html?clik=fsmain_feat1).

Linzer, Dafna. "Iran's President Does What U.S.
Diplomacy Could Not." WashingtonPost.com.
September 19, 2005. Retreived January 2006
(http://www.washingtonpost.com/wp-dyn/
content/article/2005/09/18/AR200509/
801144.html).

Moin, Baquer. *Khomeini: Life of the Ayatollah*. New
York, NY: Thomas Dunne Books, 2000.

Pollack, Kenneth M. *The Persian Puzzle: The
Conflict Between Iran and America*. New York,
NY: Random House, 2004.

"Profile: Mahmoud Ahmadinejad." BBC News.
April 28, 2006. Retrieved November 2006
(http://news.bbc.co.uk/1/hi/world/middle_east/
4107270.stm).

Sciolino, Elaine. *Persian Mirrors: The Elusive Face of
Iran*. New York, NY: Touchstone, 2000.

Simpson, John. "Iran's New Leader: A Familiar
Face?" BBC News. August 31, 2005. Retrieved

November 2006 (http://news.bbc.co.uk/2/hi/
middle_east/4626081.stm).

60 Minutes. "Iranian Leader Opens Up:
Ahmadinejad Speaks Candidly with Mike
Wallace About Israel, Nukes, Bush." CBS
News. August 13, 2006. Retrieved November
2006 (http://www.cbsnews.com/stories/2006/
08/09/60minutes/main1879867.shtml).

Takeyh, Ray. *Hidden Iran: Paradox and Power in
the Islamic Republic.* New York, NY: Times
Books, 2006.

"Timeline: Iran's Nuclear Crisis" BBC News.
September 24, 2005. Retrieved November
2006 (http://news.bbc.co.uk/2/hi/middle_east/
4134614.stm).

"Timeline: Iran's Nuclear Development."
WashingtonPost.com. 2005. Retrieved
November 2006 (http://www.washingtonpost.
com/wpdyn/content/custom/2006/01/17/
CU2006011701017.html).

"Timeline of Persian/Iranian History." On the
Matrix. Retrieved November 2006 (http://
www.on-the-matrix.com/mideast/
IranTimeline.htm).

"'Turning Point' in Iran-Iraq Ties." *Gulf-Times*.
    July 18, 2005. Retrieved November 2006
    (http://www.gulftimes.com/site/topics/article.
    asp?cu_no=2&item_no=44924&version=1&
    template_id=37&parent_id=17).

Vick, Karl. "Hard-Line Tehran Mayor Wins Iranian
    Presidency." WashingtonPost.com. June 25,
    2005. Retrieved November 2006 (http://
    www.washingtonpost.com/wpdyn/content/
    article/2005/06/24/AR2005062401696.html).

Woodruff, Bob. "Profile: Mahmoud Ahmadinejad."
    ABCNews.com. January 4, 2005. Retrieved
    November 2006 (http://abcnews.go.com/
    WNT/story?id=1471465).

Wright, Robin. *The Last Great Revolution: Turmoil
    and Transformation in Iran*. New York, NY:
    Vintage, 2001.

Index

ABOUT THE AUTHOR

Matthew Broyles has written numerous books on world politics, military affairs, and global security, including *The Six Day War* and *Air Marshals*. He studied history at Weatherford College and has published articles in a variety of print and online publications. Broyles lives in northern Texas with his wife and son.

PHOTO CREDITS

Cover, pp. 25, 39, 47, 51, 54, 56, 58, 69, 75, 78, 87, 90 © AFP/Getty Images; pp. 4–5, 17, 29, 32, 44, 61, 72, 80 © Getty Images; p. 8 Eric Lessing/Art Resource, NY; p. 11 Perry Casteñeda Library Map Collection, University of Texas at Austin; p. 12 SEF/Art Resource, NY; p. 22 © Roger Viollet/Getty Images; p. 66 © Abbas/Magnum Photos.

Designer: Evelyn Horovitz; **Photo Researcher:** Cindy Reiman